I0435119

U.S.–INDIA RELATIONS UNDER THE MODI GOVERNMENT

HEARING

BEFORE THE

SUBCOMMITTEE ON ASIA AND THE PACIFIC

OF THE

COMMITTEE ON FOREIGN AFFAIRS
HOUSE OF REPRESENTATIVES

ONE HUNDRED THIRTEENTH CONGRESS

SECOND SESSION

JULY 24, 2014

Serial No. 113–203

Printed for the use of the Committee on Foreign Affairs

Available via the World Wide Web: http://www.foreignaffairs.house.gov/ or
http://www.gpo.gov/fdsys/

U.S. GOVERNMENT PRINTING OFFICE

88–834PDF   WASHINGTON : 2014

For sale by the Superintendent of Documents, U.S. Government Printing Office
Internet: bookstore.gpo.gov   Phone: toll free (866) 512–1800; DC area (202) 512–1800
Fax: (202) 512–2104   Mail: Stop IDCC, Washington, DC 20402–0001

COMMITTEE ON FOREIGN AFFAIRS

EDWARD R. ROYCE, California, *Chairman*

CHRISTOPHER H. SMITH, New Jersey
ILEANA ROS-LEHTINEN, Florida
DANA ROHRABACHER, California
STEVE CHABOT, Ohio
JOE WILSON, South Carolina
MICHAEL T. McCAUL, Texas
TED POE, Texas
MATT SALMON, Arizona
TOM MARINO, Pennsylvania
JEFF DUNCAN, South Carolina
ADAM KINZINGER, Illinois
MO BROOKS, Alabama
TOM COTTON, Arkansas
PAUL COOK, California
GEORGE HOLDING, North Carolina
RANDY K. WEBER SR., Texas
SCOTT PERRY, Pennsylvania
STEVE STOCKMAN, Texas
RON DeSANTIS, Florida
DOUG COLLINS, Georgia
MARK MEADOWS, North Carolina
TED S. YOHO, Florida
SEAN DUFFY, Wisconsin
CURT CLAWSON, Florida

ELIOT L. ENGEL, New York
ENI F.H. FALEOMAVAEGA, American
    Samoa
BRAD SHERMAN, California
GREGORY W. MEEKS, New York
ALBIO SIRES, New Jersey
GERALD E. CONNOLLY, Virginia
THEODORE E. DEUTCH, Florida
BRIAN HIGGINS, New York
KAREN BASS, California
WILLIAM KEATING, Massachusetts
DAVID CICILLINE, Rhode Island
ALAN GRAYSON, Florida
JUAN VARGAS, California
BRADLEY S. SCHNEIDER, Illinois
JOSEPH P. KENNEDY III, Massachusetts
AMI BERA, California
ALAN S. LOWENTHAL, California
GRACE MENG, New York
LOIS FRANKEL, Florida
TULSI GABBARD, Hawaii
JOAQUIN CASTRO, Texas

AMY PORTER, *Chief of Staff*   THOMAS SHEEHY, *Staff Director*
JASON STEINBAUM, *Democratic Staff Director*

————

SUBCOMMITTEE ON ASIA AND THE PACIFIC

STEVE CHABOT, Ohio, *Chairman*

DANA ROHRABACHER, California
MATT SALMON, Arizona
MO BROOKS, Alabama
GEORGE HOLDING, North Carolina
SCOTT PERRY, Pennsylvania
DOUG COLLINS, Georgia
CURT CLAWSON, Florida

ENI F.H. FALEOMAVAEGA, American
    Samoa
AMI BERA, California
TULSI GABBARD, Hawaii
BRAD SHERMAN, California
GERALD E. CONNOLLY, Virginia
WILLIAM KEATING, Massachusetts

CONTENTS

U.S.–INDIA RELATIONS UNDER THE MODI GOVERNMENT

THURSDAY, JULY 24, 2014

House of Representatives,
Subcommittee on Asia and the Pacific,
Committee on Foreign Affairs,
Washington, DC.

The committee met, pursuant to notice, at 4 o'clock p.m., in room 2172, Rayburn House Office Building, Hon. Steve Chabot (chairman of the subcommittee) presiding.

Mr. CHABOT. The committee will come to order.

We would like to welcome everyone here and apologize for starting about an hour later than we were scheduled. We had a whole series of votes that started at the time that our committee was scheduled to start. So, we apologize for any inconvenience to anyone.

I want to start out the meeting by saying how pleased we are to have our Eni back. He is looking great, and we are certainly pleased to have him representing the other side in these hearings. Whereas, some committees, they can be at each other's throats, in this committee we tend to get along. Even if we don't necessarily agree, we do it in a nice manner. But we generally do agree on a lot of things. We are really, really happy to have Eni Faleomavaega back and we wish him great health for many years to come. And I think Ami, all kidding aside, did a very good job filling in while he was not here—really a commendable job—thank you so much, Ami, for filling in.

I also want to thank our distinguished witnesses for being here today to discuss a relationship of great importance and a country that has a great impact on the national security interests of the United States, not only in Asia, but in other parts of the world as well.

India is a nation of 1.2 billion people, and sometime in the very near future will, in all likelihood, be the most populous nation on earth, replacing China, and certainly is the powerhouse of South Asia. It has also been called an indispensable partner of the United States. This year marks the tenth anniversary of the U.S.-India Strategic Partnership, launched on January 2004 by President Bush. Over the last 10 years, we have seen this bilateral relationship evolve, and today, India is the 18th largest export market for the United States and U.S. direct investment in India has grown over 300 percent during that time. It is expected that annual bilateral trade between our two countries could increase by fivefold over the next 10 years.

In April and May, India conducted the largest democratic exercise in history. The outcome of this election was historic because the former opposition Indian People's Party, the BJP, became the first party to win a majority of India's lower chamber of Parliament since 1984 and became the first non-Congress Party to rule India's Federal Government without coalition partners. In addition, Mr. Modi is now the first lower-caste Prime Minister, the first born after the country's 1947 independence, and the first to not have been previously embedded within New Delhi's political class. We are all hopeful that the new administration will seize upon this opportunity to work with the United States in reinvigorating bilateral ties and building a more dynamic partnership.

Assistant Secretary Kumar—I think your presence here this afternoon is reflective of how important trade and investment are for the future of the U.S.-India relationship. Prime Minister Modi faces the daunting mission of reviving the Indian economy and taking steps to encourage private-sector growth. I am hopeful that his strong positions on trade and business development will help achieve this.

Initiatives to spur development in India are critical, and the U.S. can play a significant role in promoting and facilitating modernization efforts. U.S. businesses continue to face severe barriers including patent revocations, compulsory licenses, and copyright piracy, among other things. This is coupled with concerns about market access, caps on foreign direct investment, and stalled bilateral investment treaty negotiations. I hope we can hear how the administration plans to address these ongoing trade challenges, especially at the U.S.-India Strategy Dialogue next week.

I am also hopeful that Mr. Modi's resolve to implement a more assertive foreign policy will foster further geopolitical alignment and cooperation between our two nations because at the end of the day, U.S.-India strategic interests do converge more than they conflict. On the positive side, India's deepening relations with Japan pave the way for possible collaboration on efforts to respond to China's unilateral actions in the East and South China Seas. On the other hand, India's relationship with Russia and implicit support of Russian ambitions in Ukraine are concerning. I hope, Ms. Biswal, you can touch on this particular issue.

Many of my colleagues are also concerned about the persecution of religious minorities in India—largely Christian and Muslim groups—and repeated reports about discrimination against women. India has seen a 30-percent increase in incidents of communal violence since 2012, which has resulted in over 133 deaths. I hope the new Modi government makes it a priority to effectively address communal violence against all religious groups and adequately punishes rampant sexual abuse. Short of doing so, these human rights issues will only continue to impede efforts to modernize India's economy and expand opportunities for its poverty-stricken population.

As the Obama administration establishes a plan for future cooperation with India, it needs to take a leadership role in building upon U.S.-India mutual strengths, finding ways to advance mutual

3

trust, and doing a better job at helping India integrate into the international system.

While the ''Indo-Pacific Economic Corridor'' and ''New Silk Road'' are credible initiatives aimed at better integrating India with the rest of Asia, they cannot be our only efforts to do so. India must play a more prominent role in the administration's rebalance policy toward Asia because the challenges we face in the East and West do not stop at any one country's border. The new Modi administration offers us the chance to change this—to deepen cooperation across the spectrum that will harvest the region's ability to better maintain freedom of navigation, prevent the spread of terrorism, and inhibit the proliferation of nuclear weapons.

Prime Minister Modi's scheduled visit to the U.S. in September acknowledges the importance a strong U.S.-India relationship can play in our future engagement. I hope Prime Minister Modi can address and deliver on the promised reforms that are needed to strengthen ties between our two countries. And I urge the administration to be proactive in driving efforts to tackle the most salient issues that negatively affect U.S. economic and regional security interests. I again thank the witnesses for being here and look forward to their testimonies.

I would now like to turn to the gentleman from American Samoa and welcome back Eni Faleomavaega.

Mr. FALEOMAVAEGA. Thank you, Mr. Chairman.

As India's newly-elected Prime Minister Narendra Modi said, ''Good days are coming.'' And I agree.

I am grateful to our Heavenly Father for the good days and good friends. I would be remiss if I did not take this opportunity to personally thank you, Mr. Chairman and Mr. Bera, for your support, your thoughts and prayers during my time of recovery. I also thank the members of our subcommittee as well as my colleagues in the House. I am grateful to each of you and very grateful to be back working with you on important issues facing our country and the regions of Asia and the Pacific.

I believe together we still have a difference to make. And so, I thank you, Mr. Chairman, for holding this important hearing at my request on U.S.-India relations under India's newly-elected Prime Minister, my good friend Narendra Modi.

History will remember India's 2014 elections this year as unprecedented. I will remember the 2014 elections as an epic triumph because, on May 16, 2014, in the most historic election since India's independence, Shri Modi won India in a landslide victory that gave Shri Modi the most decisive mandate for an Indian Prime Minister in three decades, despite the United States using every recourse it could to disrupt his destiny.

No doubt Prime Minister Modi's destiny is to lift up the masses, assure social justice, and bring new hope for any and all who, like him, step forward and transform changes and challenges into opportunities by sheer strength of character and courage.

Prime Minister Modi's victory is India's victory. It is our victory, too. And I join with the good people of India and our Indian-American community throughout the United States in celebrating a new dawn of development for all.

Our U.S.-India partnership should be, could be, one of the most defining of the 21st century. But it is shameful that our Government, yes, the United States, failed to develop a strong friendship and comprehensive partnership with Shri Modi when it mattered most.

I thank Prime Minister Modi for accepting President Obama's invitation to meet at the White House on September 30th of this year. Prime Minister Modi's willingness to put the past in the past is a testament to his track record of good governance. He is a selfless leader who puts India and some 1.3 billion Indians first.

In recognition of his visit to our nation's Capitol, I join with my colleagues in calling upon the Speaker John Boehner and Senator Majority Leader Harry Reid to invite Prime Minster Modi to address a Joint Session of the U.S. Congress. I commend the co-chairs of the House Caucus on India and Indian Americans and their counterparts in the Senate, and also my good friends Congressman Brad Sherman, Congressman Ami Bera, Mr. Sanjay Puri of the Alliance for Indian-American Business, and all those who are working together for this purpose.

I also thank Mr. Puri for introducing me to Shri Modi in 2010, 4 years ago. In 2010, Shri Modi was Chief Minister of Gujarat and I was chairman of this subcommittee. I flew to Gujarat to meet the Chief Minister at that time at his residence. I knew then what I know now: Shri Modi is dedicated, he is determined, he is dynamic, he is different. He is the key player for improved relations between the United States and India.

Today he is the leader of the world's largest democracy, and I have every confidence he will cut across caste, creed, and religion, and bring alive the dreams of over 1 billion Indians in a world that needs his leadership. As a man of vision and action, he, together with each and every citizen of India, will create something special, an India of sustainable development and inclusive growth and an India that will rightfully assume its place in the political and economic affairs of the world.

You can be assured Prime Minister Modi will usher in India's new era, and the United States would be wise to support his goals. India will not be threatened, nor be intimidated by any country. India will deepen partnerships regionally and globally in areas of defense, nuclear energy, space research, and trade and investment. India will also invest heavily in infrastructure, affordable housing, healthcare, education, and clean energy. India will advance the interests of the developing world and lead the way in establishing a new model for maintaining stability without constraining growth. Prime Minister Modi will devote it all to eradicate poverty.

Good days are coming, Mr. Chairman. Don't matter the pundits and critics who have too long maligned Shri Modi and his supporters.

And so, once more, I congratulate Shri Modi on his path-breaking campaign, and I praise BJP Party President Singh for working shoulder-to-shoulder with Shri Modi to ensure that the spirit of democracy has triumphed.

I also commend Mr. Puri for championing the cause, the work of Shri Modi in Congress, at a time when others were not courageous enough, and for holding firm even though he was also unjustly and wrongfully maligned.

Above all, Mr. Chairman, I praise Prime Minister Modi for his beginning as a son of a tea seller to a groundbreaking victor. I wish Shri Modi every success in his historical journey forward as the Prime Minister that the people of India have long awaited.

I yield back. Thank you, Mr. Chairman.

Mr. CHABOT. Thank you very much.

We will now turn for 1 minute to other members who may want to make a statement. I will go first to Dana Rohrabacher, the gentleman from California, who is also the chairman of the Europe, Eurasia, and Emerging Threats Subcommittee.

Mr. ROHRABACHER. First and foremost, welcome back, Eni. We are grateful that you are here with us today, and that is a very good sign that we are having a hearing about our relations with India and talking about what good friends can accomplish together, because Eni and I have been working together for about 26 years now. And I feel that our friendship has helped us both accomplish some of the goals we have set out.

The same will be true with the United States and India. If there is any chance for prosperity, if there is any chance for peace and stability in large sections of this world, it will be due to a cooperative spirit and a positive relationship with India.

Mr. Modi is a breath of fresh air. Let me just note, Mr. Chairman, that we face serious challenges from folks who do not mean us well or mean the Western World well, when radical Islam and China and our central enemies happen to be the central enemies that India faces as well. We need to work together to create peace, work together to build the standard of living of the people of India and enriching our own prosperity at the same time.

So, with that said, I look forward to working with Eni and with you, Mr. Chairman, to achieve those goals and build a better relationship with India.

Mr. CHABOT. Thank you very much. The gentleman's time has expired.

The gentleman from California, Mr. Bera, is recognized for a minute to make a statement. We want to again thank him for so ably filling-in for Eni during his absence.

Mr. BERA. Thank you, Mr. Chairman.

Again, I will echo all the sentiments. I can't fill Eni's shoes, but it is great to see you back.

It is also great to see Assistant Secretary Biswal back before this committee and my fellow Californian and good friend, Assistant Secretary Kumar. It is good to see you there as well.

As an Indian-American Member of Congress and a Gujarati-American Member of Congress, this is an exciting time. I mean, there is a real time of opportunity, and I look forward to our realizing that full potential.

The last decade certainly showed us what was possible, and there is a real opportunity now for us to take this partnership to the next level. Both economically and geopolitical, India's importance is emerging in a very present way. If we do this right and we take the long view on this relationship, we really have an opportunity, as the President has said, to make this the defining relationship of the 21st century.

So, Mr. Chairman, I yield back.

Mr. CHABOT. Thank you. The gentleman yields back.

The gentleman from Pennsylvania, Mr. Perry, is recognized to make an opening statement.

Mr. PERRY. Thank you, Mr. Chairman.

Thank you, folks, for being here.

I see the great opportunities in the coming years for the bilateral relationship between the United States and India both militarily and economically. Of particular note is the immense opportunity for foreign military sales, as India is planning to spend up to $100 billion over the next decade to update its mostly Soviet Era military arsenal.

This year marks the tenth anniversary of the U.S.-India Strategic Partnership, which was launched in January 2004 by then-President George Bush. I look forward to hearing an assessment from our distinguished witnesses of this bilateral relationship over the past decade and how they see this relationship evolving over the coming decades.

And I yield back.

Mr. CHABOT. Thank you. The gentleman yields back.

The gentleman from California, Mr. Sherman, is recognized for 1 minute, he is also the ranking member of the Terrorism, Nonproliferation, and Trade Subcommittee.

Mr. SHERMAN. Thank you.

It is great to have Eni back.

Thank you for distributing these CDs. And let me assure my colleagues that I will not be putting out anything similar. [Laughter.]

Mr. CHABOT. Noted for the record here.

Mr. SHERMAN. We have just seen an election in India in which some 550 million people participated. That is the greatest exercise of the franchise in the history of the world.

For that and so many other reasons, Mr. Faleomavaega, Mr. Poe, and myself have been circulating a letter—we now have 84 of our colleagues to join us in the effort—to congressional leadership saying that we ought to have Mr. Modi address a Joint Session of Congress.

Finally, as to the nuclear agreement, I will hope to learn in these hearings whether India will adopt the liability protections that will allow American companies to participate. In light of Bhopal, I can see why that might be politically difficult in India. But, as a practical matter, India will benefit from the additional competition to allow U.S. companies to compete along with those companies that already enjoy sovereign immunity.

And I yield back.

Mr. CHABOT. Thank you. The gentleman yields back.

The gentleman from North Carolina, Mr. Holding, is recognized for 1 minute.

Mr. HOLDING. Thank you very much, Mr. Chairman.

There can be no question that now is the time for relations between the United States and India to be taken to the next level. Having visited India just last year, I have no doubt that the U.S.-India relationship can be made into one of the defining partnerships of this century. Joining up the Modi magic with the American dream would be a very powerful combination worldwide.

Mr. Chairman, with any partnership there is always room for improvement. For the United States and India to fully recognize the opportunity that exists right now, progress must be made to address concerns with India's intellectual property system and other domestic laws and requirements that have been a concern for a number of U.S. companies doing business there.

And for our part, Mr. Chairman, Congress must reject ill-conceived immigration proposals in the Senate that would harm successful collaboration between the U.S. and India companies. We must also mend relations with the Prime Minister that were damaged with the denial of his visa prior to being elected.

It is not a small secret, Mr. Chairman, that our relationship with India over the last few years has not been as engaged as it could be or should have been. And I look forward to discussing what steps we can take to remedy this and capture the opportunity presented to us here for a new day with India and the United States.

Thank you, and I yield back.

Mr. CHABOT. Thank you very much. The gentleman's time has expired.

I would also like to thank our newest member of this committee, Curt Clawson, who is from the 19th district of Florida, speaks four languages, and all kinds of other great stuff. I will now yield to the gentleman either to talk about India or, if you would like to, talk about yourself. You have 1 minute.

Mr. CLAWSON. This is a Samoan CD. I would say my favorite movies from foreign are Telugu, Film Nagar, Hyderabad. I went to school with Nagarjuna. I know Jagapathi. And these are my friends. I love Hyderabad. I love Chennai. And I am very familiar with your country.

I have also run businesses with Mr. Kalyani in Bharat Forge, three factories for a joint venture in Pune.

I am familiar with your country. I love your country, and I am hopeful with the new change in regime that the future and the land of promise and the land of opportunity of India can finally become so.

And I understand the complications of so many languages and so many cultures and so many histories, all rolled up in one. But this is an awesome country with awesome potential and somebody that we need to be friends with and that we can trust, not just for security, but what is also important to me is for economic development. As was said earlier, technology and technology protection is I think a big issue in that.

So, I am enthusiastic about working with you all, and anything that I can do to make the relationship with India better, I am willing and enthusiastic about doing so.

Thank you. I yield back.

Mr. CHABOT. Thank you very much.

I will now introduce the panel, the distinguished panelists this afternoon, both of whom really need no introduction, but I am going to do it anyway.

Nisha Biswal was sworn in as Assistant Secretary of State for South and Central Asian Affairs last October. Previously, Ms.

Biswal served as the Assistant Administrator for Asia at USAID. During Ms. Biswal's tenure USAID reopened its mission in Burma and transitioned its programs in various countries to global partnerships in development cooperation. Ms. Biswal also worked in the Office of U.S. Foreign Disaster Assistance and the Office of Transition Initiatives, and served as Chief of Staff in the Management Bureau while at USAID. Before USAID, Ms. Biswal served as the majority clerk for the House Appropriations Foreign Operations Subcommittee and as professional staff for the House Foreign Affairs Committee, where she was responsible for South Asia. Ms. Biswal has also worked at InterAction and at the American Red Cross, where she served as the International Delegate in Armenia, Georgia, and Azerbaijan. And we welcome you back to the committee.

I would also like to introduce Arun M. Kumar. Mr. Kumar has served as Assistant Secretary of Commerce for Global Markets and Director General of the U.S. and Foreign Commercial Service since March of this year. In this role, he leads the trade and investment promotion efforts for the U.S. Government. Mr. Kumar has extensive global experience in the business world. Prior to his nomination, he was a partner and member of the Board of Directors at KPMG, LLP. He led the firm's West Coast Management Consulting practice, serving major global clients as well emerging Silicon Valley ventures. He also found and led KPMG's U.S.-India practice. Previously, Mr. Kumar was a Silicon Valley entrepreneur and has acted as a mentor and advisor to several new ventures in Silicon Valley and India. He has served on the advisory councils at Stanford University and the University of California, Santa Cruz, and he is on the Board of Directors of the U.S.-India Business Council.

We welcome you here this afternoon, Mr. Kumar.

I know both of the witnesses are familiar with the committee rules. You both will have 5 minutes. There is a lighting system. The yellow light will let you know you have 1 minute. When the red light comes on, we would ask you to wrap up as closely as possible. We do give a little leeway, but not much.

So, Ms. Biswal, you are recognized for 5 minutes.

STATEMENT OF THE HONORABLE NISHA BISWAL, ASSISTANT SECRETARY, BUREAU OF SOUTH AND CENTRAL ASIAN AFFAIRS, U.S. DEPARTMENT OF STATE

Ms. BISWAL. Thank you very much, Mr. Chairman.

Chairman Chabot, Ranking Member Faleomavaega, thank you for having this hearing and inviting me to testify today.

I want to just echo the sentiments on the dais about how wonderful it is to see you again sitting on the dais, Mr. Faleomavaega.

It is a wonderful time to have this hearing and an important time to have this hearing. I am glad to be here with my good friend Arun Kumar.

In the interest of time, I am going to summarize the points which all of you have made so eloquently on the importance of the relationship and the opportunity we have, and ask that my full statement be entered for the record.

Mr. CHABOT. Without objection, so ordered.

Ms. BISWAL. Thank you, Mr. Chairman.

There is no better time than now to reexamine the U.S.-India relationship. The historic elections, as you have noted, this spring conferred an unprecedented mandate on Prime Minister Narendra Modi and his party, and also created an historic opportunity for the United States and India to re-energize our relationship.

Deputy Secretary Bill Burns and I traveled to New Delhi 2 weeks ago to meet with Prime Minister Modi and key members of his cabinet. Secretary Kerry will travel soon to India to co-chair the next round of our Strategic Dialogue, and he will be joined by Secretary of Commerce Pritzker in underscoring the vital role of our economic partnership.

Mr. Chairman, the Obama administration's rebalance to Asia is a strategic bet on the consequential role of Asia's 4.3 billion people in the 21st century and Asia's growing importance to America's security and prosperity. But, for Asia to comprise 50 percent of global GDP, as many project, its citizens and governments must make the right choices to foster sustainable and inclusive growth, to promote open and free trade, and to combat terrorism and extremism.

In all of these areas, India has a vital role to play. Its rise as a regional and global power, its economic and strategic growth are deeply in the U.S. interest, as has been noted by members on the dais. Like the United States, India increasingly sees its future in a secure, connected, and prosperous Asia Pacific. We not only share democratic values, but also a deep interest in a peaceful and rules-based order.

But, if India is to achieve its potential, it will need to address myriad economic and governance challenges. Much of the excitement that the new Modi government has generated in India, around the world, and, most notably, in the business community, has been around this idea of accountable and effective government that can unleash India's economic potential.

While my colleague will discuss our economic and trade partnership in greater depth, I just want to underscore that our economies, our businesses, our universities, and our people can partner in helping India realize sustained and inclusive growth and enjoy a vision of shared prosperity.

Our trade has already grown fivefold since the year 2000 to almost $100 billion annually. We can grow that fivefold again in the years to come. And we are committed to addressing the inevitable frictions over trade through dialogue and engagement.

Our energy cooperation, one of the brightest areas of the partnership, is helping India meet its growing energy needs and creating opportunities for our businesses through contracts for export of American LNG and fulfilling the promise of delivering cutting-edge nuclear energy technology, as well as collaboration on clean energy solutions.

But, as I noted at the outset, the locus of our convergent strategic interests is across the Asian landscape. When Prime Minister Modi invited regional leaders to his inauguration, he demonstrated his commitment to strengthening India's ties within its immediate region. And we see a partnership with India that spans east, west, north, and south, to advance our shared interests across the Indo-Pacific Region.

Our collaboration on counterterrorism and homeland security has grown tremendously in the past several years and has already helped to bring to justice several of the terrorists in the Mumbai attacks. We are committed to further strengthening this robust cooperation in order to protect both our nations and both our peoples.

Defense cooperation continues to play a vital role in our partnership, which Secretary Hagel's visit to India in early August will help to underscore. The breadth and depth of military exchanges and exercises have grown tremendously, and the Indian navy is participating in the RIMPAC Maritime Security Exercise in Honolulu for the first time this year.

Additionally, as we speak today, we have begun our joint naval exercise, the Malabar, and this year, also, with the participation of Japan, this is a great example of our trilateral cooperation and a manifestation of the U.S.-India-Japan trilateral dialogue.

These military ties are complemented also by our growing defense trade. We are overcoming bureaucratic hurdles and paving the way to increase defense trade and potential for co-production and co-development.

Mr. Chairman, the true potential of this relationship was best characterized by Prime Minister Modi himself when he said to us 2 weeks ago that it is not just benefits to the Indian people and the American people, but that the true value of the U.S.-India relationship is that, when the world's oldest democracy and the world's largest democracy come together, it is the world that stands to benefit.

We deeply appreciate the strong support of the U.S. Congress and of this committee as well as members in the Senate and the House and the Indian Caucus in advancing the U.S.-India partnership. We look forward to closely collaborating with you in the years ahead, as we forge an ever-increasingly closer partnership between our two countries.

Thank you, Mr. Chairman, and I will conclude my remarks here and look forward to answering any questions that you or the committee may have.

[The prepared statement of Ms. Biswal follows:]

WRITTEN STATEMENT

TESTIMONY BEFORE THE HOUSE FOREIGN AFFAIRS COMMITTEE
SUBCOMMITTEE ON ASIA AND THE PACIFIC
NISHA D. BISWAL
ASSISTANT SECRETARY OF STATE
BUREAU OF SOUTH AND CENTRAL ASIAN AFFAIRS

"U.S.-India Relations Under the Modi Government"

July 24, 2014

Chairman Chabot, Ranking Member Faleomavaega, thank you for inviting me to testify before you today. It is an honor to appear before this Committee, and I am pleased to speak alongside my colleague, Assistant Secretary for Global Markets at the Commerce Department Arun Kumar.

There is no better time than now to re-examine U.S.-India relations. The historic elections this spring, which brought a record 530 million Indians to the ballot box, conferred an unprecedented mandate on Prime Minister Narendra Modi and the Bharatiya Janata Party. Those elections also created a historic opportunity for the United States and India to re-energize our relationship.

Mr. Chairman, the Obama administration's rebalance to Asia is a strategic bet on the consequential role of Asia's 4.3 billion people in the 21st century. This region already accounts for a quarter of global GDP – and this could grow to one-half by 2050. But that will only be possible if the citizens and governments of Asia make the right choices – to foster sustainable and inclusive growth, to promote open and free trade, and to combat terrorism and extremism.

In all of these areas, India has a vital role to play, in South Asia, in the Asia-Pacific, and, increasingly, on the global stage. India's rise as a regional and global leader, and its economic and strategic growth, are deeply in the U.S. interest. Through its "Look East" policy, India is increasingly engaged with Southeast Asia and East Asia. With the opening in Burma, those connections, whether economic, political, or people-to-people, will only grow. That is why we are making the strategic bet on India's rise. Like the United States, India increasingly sees its future in a secure, connected, and prosperous Asia-Pacific. We share not only democratic values but also a deep interest in a peaceful, rules-based order in the Asia-Pacific. Our partnership is already strong, whether in strengthening maritime security and disaster response (including through our trilateral cooperation with Japan), combating terrorism in South Asia, or developing innovative development and health solutions. As we look to the opportunities and challenges of the future, we think this partnership will become even more vital, as we work together to grow our economic relationship for the shared prosperity of both our peoples, advance connectivity across the Indo-Pacific, and address shared challenges such as climate change. Put simply, the United States and India are more invested than ever in each other.

I accompanied Deputy Secretary Bill Burns to India two weeks ago to meet with Prime Minister Modi and key members of his cabinet to discuss their economic and security agenda as well as the U.S.-India relationship. The Modi government has identified infrastructure, manufacturing, modernizing the military, energy security, attracting greater foreign investment, and expanding access to skills training and education as key priorities. For India to achieve its potential, the Prime Minister has said that one of his top priorities will be efficient, effective, and accountable governance.

In all the areas that the Modi government has identified as priorities, we think the United States, including our businesses and universities, can play an important role in helping address the challenges India faces and creating opportunities that benefit both countries. But the true potential of the relationship is best captured in what Prime Minister Modi said to Deputy Secretary Burns during our visit. He noted that he does not see our relations in terms of the benefits it brings to the Indian people or the American people – that goes without saying. The true power and potential of this relationship, he said, is that when the world's oldest democracy and the world's largest democracy come together, the world will benefit.

Mr. Chairman, it is in that vein that Secretary Kerry and Commerce Secretary Pritzker will travel to India next week, to hold the first U.S.-India Strategic Dialogue with the new government. We will focus on shared prosperity and strategic convergence – more specifically, how partnership between the United States and India can make our countries and the entire global order more prosperous and more secure.

ECONOMIC AND TRADE PARTNERSHIP

While my colleague will discuss our economic and trade partnership with India in greater depth, I would like to briefly touch upon a few aspects of this important relationship.

Our two countries have never been more invested in each other's economic future. India's goal of building a strong and integrated economy that is led by private-sector growth and boasts a global reach will offer sustainable, long-term market opportunities for U.S. firms. American companies recognize the tremendous potential of India's economy and are eager to make long-term investments in India. U.S. companies – boasting the highest standards and highest-quality products and services – can play an invaluable role in transforming the Indian economy through partnerships for joint innovation and development. Cross-pollination of U.S. and Indian businesses is a win-win for our economies and will create thousands of jobs in both our countries.

A vital part of our economic agenda is higher education. Indian students comprise the second-largest group of foreign students in the United States, with 100,000 students studying in the United States in 2012-13. Not only do they contribute over $3 billion to the U.S. economy every year, they also advance innovation and research in our universities and contribute to the diversity and vibrancy of campuses. Working with the Indian government, we are also helping India adapt our community college model to meet its skills needs and goal of building 10,000 community colleges by 2030, so that India's future workforce can benefit from one of our nation's greatest exports, knowledge and skill development.

To fully realize its economic potential, India also needs to foster inclusive and sustainable growth. While women continue to rise to the highest positions in civil society, business, and government, in many ways the potential of women and girls in India remains untapped and underutilized as a force for growth and development. Fundamental issues of women's security and opportunity need to be addressed, so that Indian women can achieve their full potential and make their contribution to India's growth story.

Climate change is another issue that all emerging economies, including India, are grappling with. For growth to be enduring, it must be environmentally sustainable. We enjoy a broad range of bilateral cooperation with India on clean energy and climate issues, including Secretary Kerry's Climate Change Working Group. Our cooperation on mitigating the causes and effects of climate change, including investment in and development of clean and renewable energy sources, is increasingly a whole-of-government effort. It is our hope this bilateral cooperation can lead to greater collaboration in multilateral fora.

ENERGY AND INNOVATION

We have seen tremendous progress in our energy cooperation since the launch of the U.S.-India Energy Dialogue in 2005. This forum has brought our governments and private sectors together to expand cooperation on nuclear energy, electrical grid and power generation, energy efficiency, and oil and gas exploration. It has also expanded markets for renewable energy technologies and lowered barriers to clean energy deployment. The Energy Dialogue – along with the Energy Security Roundtable – has leveraged each country's strengths in research, opened opportunities for American businesses and technologies, and strengthened India's energy security and economic growth. We are working together to further deepen our energy relationship, through the expansion of contracts for the export of American liquefied natural gas, identification of unconventional energy resources; and fulfilling the promise of delivering cutting-edge U.S. nuclear energy technology to meet Indian energy needs.

One fast-growing area of partnership is our robust science and technology cooperation. We will showcase one facet of our technology partnership later this year in New Delhi at the U.S.-India Technology Summit, which will enable the establishment of new partnerships in innovation and technology development stemming from breakthroughs our scientists and engineers have achieved together. Already, our two countries are deploying a rotavirus vaccine, ROTAVAC, the product of a public-private partnership that has the potential to save hundreds of thousands of young lives in India and around the world. Our collaboration sustains economic growth and job creation while helping our citizens live longer, healthier lives.

NASA has also collaborated with the Indian Space Research Organization to share navigation expertise for India's Mars Orbiter Mission, and we are exploring even more opportunities for collaboration through our Civil Space Joint Working Group.

SECURITY

Our security engagement is central to the U.S.-India partnership. We are committed to a strong and influential India in the security realm. India is a regional and emerging global power, as well as a provider of security and a strategic partner with shared interests from the Indian Ocean to Afghanistan and beyond.

India remains an active and strong CT partner. Our cooperation has already brought to justice several Mumbai terrorists. As President Obama has stated, the Mumbai perpetrators, financers, and sponsors must be held accountable for their crimes. We will also continue to work together to track and disrupt terrorism, including those responsible for the Indian consulate attack in Herat.

Our military-to-military ties are strong and growing. India is participating in the Rim-of-the-Pacific (RIMPAC) 2014 exercise in Hawaii, where for the first time an Indian frigate has joined this large multilateral activity. Japan will participate in MALABAR, our largest bilateral naval exercise with India, which in fact began today and runs through July 30.

Defense cooperation continues to play a significant role in advancing the strategic partnership. One of the pillars of our effort to build a strategic partnership with India on defense issues is the U.S.-India Defense Trade and Technology Initiative, which has helped us overcome bureaucratic hurdles and paved the way for increased private-sector ties, science and technology cooperation, defense trade, and potential for co-production and co-development. We hope to see more partnerships take root, like the one between Lockheed Martin and Tata building C-130 components in Hyderabad. We will continue to look for opportunities to foster closer ties between the U.S. and Indian defense sectors, and to advocate on behalf of U.S. industry for needed changes in the Indian system, such as continued reforms to their offset system. We are encouraged by the Modi government's proposal in the budget introduced earlier this month to raise FDI caps in the defense sector to 49 per cent.

REGIONAL COOPERATION

As I noted at the outset, a strong Indian leadership role is deeply in the U.S. interest. In inviting regional leaders to his inauguration, Prime Minister Modi signaled that India will play a greater strategic role in its immediate neighborhood and across the Indo-Pacific region, which we strongly support. We see great potential for expanding connectivity and trade across an Indo-Pacific Economic Corridor. The fact that India trades more with Europe, the United States, and the Middle East than with its immediate South Asian neighbors is a global economic anomaly, one that India can help address by shaping a connectivity network between India, South Asia, and the rest of the continent.

We support increasing trade and investment between India and Pakistan, and reducing trade barriers. That will advance both nations' prosperity and strengthen peace and stability. Further west, India shares our goal of a successful transformation in Afghanistan. We both want to ensure the peace and stability of a democratic Afghanistan, and help it economically integrate further into the South and Central Asia region through our New Silk Road strategy. We have further expanded our regional consultations with India to include South, Central, West, and East Asia. These consultations are not just a talk shop: The U.S.-India-Japan trilateral dialogue, for example, has deepened our partnership on our Indo-Pacific Economic Corridor agenda, maritime security, humanitarian assistance and disaster planning, as well as coordination in multilateral fora. Last year, with the support of India, we participated in the Indian Ocean Regional Association as a dialogue partner for the first time.

LOOKING AHEAD

Our bilateral engagements over the next several months will reinforce our strategic, economic, and people-to-people ties. The Strategic Dialogue will kick off a series of high-level visits throughout the late summer and fall, culminating in the visit of Prime Minister Modi to Washington at the invitation of the President. We think this is a time of tremendous potential for the U.S.-India partnership. By reinvigorating this partnership and setting ambitious new goals for the future, we are making future generations of Americans and Indians safer and more prosperous and helping strengthen stability in Asia and around the world.

Mr. Chairman, let me take this opportunity to thank you for the strong support of the U.S. Congress and this committee in particular for the U.S.-India partnership. The advocacy and support for this relationship, by members of both houses and from both parties, has been one of its sources of strength. I look forward to working closely with you as we embark on a new chapter of U.S.-India relations in the months and years to come.

Thank you, Mr. Chairman. I look forward to answering any questions that you and others from the Committee may have.

Mr. CHABOT. Thank you very much.

Mr. Kumar, you are recognized for 5 minutes.

STATEMENT OF THE HONORABLE ARUN KUMAR, DIRECTOR GENERAL OF THE U.S. AND FOREIGN COMMERCIAL SERVICE AND ASSISTANT SECRETARY FOR GLOBAL MARKETS, INTERNATIONAL TRADE ADMINISTRATION, U.S. DEPARTMENT OF COMMERCE

Mr. KUMAR. Chairman Chabot, Ranking Member Faleomavaega, and members of the subcommittee, thank you for the opportunity to speak about the Department of Commerce's engagement with India. I am honored to be here alongside my friend and colleague from the State Department, Assistant Secretary Nisha Biswal.

The Department's International Trade Administration is the agency responsible for promoting U.S. exports, expanding markets overseas, and enforcing U.S. trade laws. Our efforts are driven by the needs of our primary constituency, the U.S. business community.

In 2010, President Obama said the U.S.-India relationship will be ''one of the defining partnerships of the 21st century.'' While India is a large market, our commercial relationship remains underdeveloped relative to its potential. With the new government in charge, the timing may be right to improve our bilateral trade relationship.

From 2000 to 2013, U.S.-India two-way trade has grown from $19 billion in goods and services to about $97 billion. Having recently returned from India, I will agree that the potential is, indeed, vast.

ITA understands the value of exports and its direct correlation to job growth. Our staff in 100 locations across the country and in over 75 markets around the world is dedicated to helping companies enter new markets and expanding current ones.

In India, our staffing is currently strategically placed with a total of seven posts, making it the largest footprint of any ITA operation outside the U.S. Furthermore, ITA's Advocacy Center, which coordinates U.S. Government commercial advocacy, helps U.S. companies win foreign government contracts. Between 2010 and 2013, ITA recorded advocacy wins in India with estimated contract values of $5.2 billion.

Another focus of ITA is to encourage inward investment, and the Obama administration created SelectUSA, the only U.S. Governmentwide program to attract, retain, and grow business investment in the United States. In 2012, India's stock of foreign investment into the U.S. totaled roughly $9 billion. Last year we hosted the first SelectUSA Investment Summit, and India was one of the largest delegations with 39 participants. Based on the success of this event, SelectUSA is organizing a second summit in March 2015.

Doing business internationally can be risky, and India comes with its fair share of challenges. There are many areas that hinder us from deepening our trade relationship with India. U.S. companies need to be aware of these obstacles before entering the Indian market.

These include protection and enforcement of intellectual property rights, localization requirements, high tariffs, and a difficult regulatory system that lacks transparency and predictability. ITA works to resolve these issues in a variety of ways.

First, we lead the public-private U.S.-India Commercial Dialogue. The dialogue has been effective in facilitating information exchanges between government and private sector experts on standards and regulatory procedures.

Second, ITA chairs working groups on biotechnology, life sciences, civil aviation, and infrastructure in the High Technology Cooperation Group, led by Commerce's Bureau of Industry and Security.

We also support the State Department and USTR in the technical discussions on a U.S.-India bilateral investment treaty.

ITA also organizes trade missions and trade events, provides market research, counseling, and customized support to companies looking to export to India. In 2015, the Department is organizing a trade mission to introduce U.S. firms to India's rapidly-expanding ports and marine technology market.

On the domestic side, ITA ensures U.S. companies enjoy fair competition here at home. Our agency is responsible for administering the U.S. antidumping and countervailing duty laws. As of today, we have 22 orders in place against a variety of Indian products.

As I have expressed throughout this testimony, the United States remains actively engaged in India. The Commerce Department and ITA will continue to expand our contacts with a new government in New Delhi, the state governments where so many decisions are now made, and with U.S. and Indian businesses in order to promote exports of U.S. goods and services.

Today we just announced that Secretary Pritzker will be joining Secretary Kerry at the upcoming U.S.-India Strategic Dialogue scheduled for July 31 in Delhi. We will use this meeting and other opportunities to grow our commercial relationship.

Thank you for the opportunity to speak with you today. I will welcome your questions.

[The prepared statement of Mr. Kumar follows:]

Written Testimony

Statement of Arun Kumar
Assistant Secretary of Commerce for Global Markets and
Director General of the U.S. and Foreign Commercial Service
International Trade Administration
U.S. Department of Commerce
Before
The House of Representatives Committee on Foreign Affairs
Subcommittee on Asia and the Pacific

"U.S.-India Relations under the Modi Government"
July 24, 2014

<u>Introduction</u>

Chairman Chabot, Ranking Member Faleomavaega, and members of the Subcommittee, thank you for the opportunity to speak about the Department of Commerce's role in promoting U.S. business abroad along with increasing investment into the United States and specifically our engagement with India.

The Department of Commerce's International Trade Administration (ITA) strengthens the competitiveness of U.S. industry, promotes trade and investment and ensures fair trade through the rigorous enforcement of our trade laws and agreements. ITA's efforts are driven by the needs of our primary constituency – the U.S. business community.

India is a huge country with an enormous market that significantly underperforms in the context of its commercial relationship with the United States. With a new government in charge, the timing may be right to materially improve our bilateral trade relationship, which could translate into greater opportunities for U.S. businesses. Despite all of the economic and commercial challenges we face in India, it is an important global partner and key player in the region.

In 2010, President Obama said the United States-India relationship will be "one of the defining partnerships of the 21st century" and that the United States "seek[s] prosperity – a strong and growing economy in an open international economic system."[1]

---

[1] *Remarks by the President to the Joint Session of the Indian Parliament in New Delhi, India,* November 8, 2010, http://www.whitehouse.gov/the-press-office/2010/11/08/remarks-president-joint-session-indian-parliament-new-delhi-india

From 2000-2013, United States-India trade in goods and services has grown from $19 billion annually to $97 billion. Having recently returned from India where I met senior Government of India (GoI) officials, chambers of commerce, and leaders of U.S. and Indian businesses, I would agree that the potential is indeed vast.

A U.S.-India Strategic Dialogue (SD) meeting is scheduled for July 31, 2014 with the participation of Secretary of State Kerry and Secretary of Commerce Pritzker. The Dialogue will build on the newly elected Prime Minister Modi's agenda to return India to robust and sustainable economic growth.

The Importance of India

The commercial importance of India to the United States is growing: it is the world's third largest economy (after the United States and China) measured by GDP in terms of purchasing power parity ($6.78 trillion in 2013), the tenth largest in nominal GDP ($1.88 trillion), and the eighth largest consumer economy.[2] It has an urban middle class forecasted to reach 400 million people and a significant "affluent class," both of which translate into high-potential markets for U.S. exporters.

India is currently a relatively small market for the United States, in terms of total U.S. exports, highlighting the potential opportunity for continued growth. Manufactured goods such as diamonds, gold, and jewelry; aircraft and aircraft parts; and machinery are among the leading products that the United States exports to India. (See table below.)

Top U.S. Goods Exports to India in 2013

Product	Value of Exports in $	Share of Total U.S. Goods Exports to India
Diamonds, Gold, and Jewelry	$5.8 billion	26.4%
Aircraft and Parts	$3.0 billion	13.5%
Machinery	$2.2 billion	10.3%
Electrical Machinery	$1.3 billion	6.0%
Medical, Analytical, and Measuring and Checking Instruments	$1.3 billion	5.9%

---

[2] World Bank Indicators for 2013: GDP (Current US$); and GDP, PPP (current international $); and Household final consumption expenditure (current US$).

Carbon Black, Coal, Petroleum Coke, and Petroleum Oils	$1.3 billion	5.8%
India Total	*$21.8 billion*	*1.4% (Share of U.S. goods exports to the world)*
World	*$1,579.6 billion*	--

Source: Census Bureau, Global Trade Atlas (accessed June 30, 2014)

Top U.S. Services Exports to India in 2013

Service	Value of Exports in $	Share of Total U.S. Services Exports to India
Travel (for all purposes including education)	$7.3 billion	54.4%
Transport	$2.0 billion	14.7%
Other business services	$1.1 billion	7.9%
Telecommunications, computer, and information services	$961 million	7.1%
Charges for the use of intellectual property not included elsewhere	$890 million	6.6%
Financial services	$567 million	4.2%
Maintenance and repair services not included elsewhere	$332 million	2.5%
Government goods and services not included elsewhere	$270 million	2.0%
Insurance services	$88 million	0.7%
India Total	*$13.5 billion*	*2.0% (Share of U.S. services exports to the world)*
World	*$687.4 billion*	--

*Source: U.S. Bureau of Economic Analysis, *Table 1.3. U.S. International Transactions, Expanded Detail by Area and Country;* and *Table 1.1, U.S. International Transactions* (for U.S. exports to world). Release date June 18, 2014 for both tables.

A priority for ITA is to expand commercial opportunities for U.S. exporters in India through the promotion of U.S. exports of goods and services and improved access to the Indian market.

Another priority is to increase direct investment in the United States from India. These efforts are part of a broader Administration effort to increase prosperity in both countries and complement bilateral efforts to enhance regional and global security. This ultimately strengthens democracy and civil society around the world.

ITA's presence in India, with a total of seven posts (New Delhi, Ahmedabad, Bangalore, Chennai, Hyderabad, Kolkata, and Mumbai), gives it the largest footprint of any ITA operation outside the United States in terms of number of locations in one country. In Ahmedabad and Bangalore, the Commercial Service is the only U.S. Government agency present and supports the U.S. Mission in India as a whole. In cooperation with local Indian business chambers, we operate 13 American Business Corners (ABCs) in second- and third-tier cities in every region of India to promote U.S. goods and services exports as broadly as possible. Since we opened the first ABCs in 2012, they have recorded 60 export success stories and one foreign direct investment success.

Supporting U.S. Companies

ITA understands the value of exports and its direct correlation to job growth. ITA plays a vital role in the needs of American companies seeking to do business in India. The Indian subcontinent is one of the largest and most diverse markets served by ITA. ITA, through its U.S. and Foreign Commercial Service (Commercial Service), whose mission includes to help U.S. companies enter new markets and expand exports in current ones, currently has staff in over 100 cities in the United States and at U.S. Embassies and Consulates in over 75 markets around the world.

ITA's Commercial Service in India currently has 63 employees, including ten Foreign Service Officers and 53 locally-employed staff. They are located in seven offices which provide broad geographic coverage in a varied and decentralized market. The India-based Commercial Service staff also includes Officers supporting two other Commerce Department bureaus (Patent and Trademark Office and the Bureau of Industry and Security), raising the total Commerce staff count to 72.

The geographic dispersion of the Commercial Service's India-based staff reflects the decentralized way business is conducted in India and accounts for the strong and influential role of India's 29 States. While the potential for export sales into such a vast market is striking, the challenges in India are significant, and ITA will continue to explore opportunities for improved market access for U.S. businesses with the new Government of India. ITA's proactive support for U.S. firms exporting to India helps American companies become more competitive in the Indian market.

ITA maintains staff at the Asian Development Bank (ADB) in the Philippines where we provide information to U.S. companies on projects funded by the ADB. India is the biggest borrower from the ADB in the region as its infrastructure needs are substantial. This year, Commercial Service India began developing a closer working relationship with ADB staff. The demand for infrastructure growth in India will increase the demands for capital and ITA stands ready to help U.S. exporters tap into these projects as they come online.

ITA also runs the Advocacy Center, which coordinates U.S. Government advocacy for small, medium, and large U.S. companies in various sectors to assist in winning government contracts across the globe. In regards to India, between FY 2010 and 2013, ITA recorded advocacy wins with estimated contract values of $5.2 billion and U.S. export content of $5.0 billion. So far in FY 2014, we have successfully helped U.S. companies win $4.2 billion in contracts, all of which was U.S. content. The Advocacy Center currently has $30.9 billion in proposed contracts in the India portfolio, including $15.1 billion in U.S. export content, for which the U.S. Government is an advocate abroad.

Meeting the Challenges of Doing Business

Doing business internationally can be risky and confusing for companies, particularly the small- and medium-sized enterprises that are at the core of ITA's mission. ITA's policy efforts are geared toward improving short-, medium- and long-term successes in international commerce. We do this in four ways: 1) by providing direct support to U.S. companies, using existing tools and relationships to help resolve commercial problems; 2) by opening markets and working with foreign governments to improve the business climate; 3) by representing U.S. business interests during trade negotiations; and 4) by helping to enforce our current trade agreements.

As noted previously, India is our 18th-largest goods export market, and the United States-India commercial relationship holds great potential for growth. However, the current level of U.S. exports is actually rather small for a market of India's size. There are many issues that limit our trade from reaching that potential. U.S. companies need to be aware of and vigilant about these issues before attempting to enter the Indian market. These include protection and enforcement of intellectual property rights (IPR); localization requirements; high tariffs and other import charges; market access barriers for certain services sectors; a difficult regulatory and bureaucratic system that often lacks transparency and predictability; and corruption.

ITA provides direct support for real-time business needs; its goal is to monitor and work with other U.S. agencies to ensure that India implements and adheres to its trade agreement obligations and otherwise affords market access for U.S. exports. ITA uses its close relationship with U.S. industry, as well as its understanding of India's political, cultural and business climate, to ensure that India is fulfilling its obligations and that our companies are able to compete with domestic firms in that country. Our network of foreign and domestic commercial officers, locally-employed staff, and industry experts in Washington, D.C and trade specialists around the country work closely with U.S. firms to help them overcome barriers to doing business in foreign markets.

Let me highlight some key initiatives where ITA plays a critical role to facilitate U.S. companies' success in the Indian market.

ITA leads the public-private U.S.-India Commercial Dialogue (CD). The CD has been effective in facilitating information exchanges between government and private-sector experts on standards and regulatory procedures. In March, we renewed the CD for its eighth two-year term. ITA also chairs working groups on biotechnology, life sciences and civil aviation and infrastructure in the public-private High Technology Cooperation Group led by Commerce's Bureau of Industry and Security. ITA has chaired the working group on industrial tariffs and non-tariff barriers under the Trade Policy Forum led by the Office of the U.S. Trade Representative (USTR). We are supporting the technical discussions on a bilateral investment treaty (BIT) with the Indian Government that are led by USTR and the State Department. A BIT could provide added confidence to investors, deepen our economic relationship, and support job creation and economic growth in both countries.

Linking U.S. Business with Buyers Overseas and Attracting Investment Back Home

ITA provides numerous tools to help U.S. companies learn more about the Indian market, and meet potential clients, distributors, and partners. ITA organizes trade missions and trade events, and provides market research, export counseling and customized support to companies looking to export to India. In fact, the Commerce Department is organizing an executive-led trade mission to India in February 2015. The mission will introduce U.S. firms to India's rapidly expanding ports and marine technology market. Given the new Government of India priorities in infrastructure (Rail, Roads, Power, Ports, Airports, Water and Energy), the Department is re-doubling its efforts to increase U.S. exports and to align them with the priorities identified by the Government of India.

As demonstrated in the table below, each year ITA's customers are reporting more export successes by new-to-market clients in India. Since 2010, more and more U.S. companies have been exporting to India.

Year	Export Successes	New-to-Market Clients
2010	464	121
2011	498	144
2012	470	185
2013	763	401

ITA prides itself on helping U.S. companies, especially small and medium-sized enterprises (SMEs). For example, Avazzia, Inc., a Dallas-based SME manufacturer of electro-stimulating pain management devices, contacted its local U.S. Export Assistance Center with the goal of selling its products and services in India's growing healthcare market. The Mumbai Commercial Service office provided a Gold Key Service to Avazzia, that is, our in-country ITA staff researched the local market and arranged face-to-face meetings for the company with numerous potential distributors and agents in India. Since receiving these services, Avazzia Inc. has entered into a distributorship agreement with a Mumbai-based company and shipped its first order to India, recording a new-to-market success.

Enforcing Domestic Trade Laws

ITA is in charge of enforcing the antidumping duty (AD) and countervailing duty (CVD) laws, and also has statutory authority to monitor trade agreement compliance.[3] Through enforcement of trade remedy laws and ensuring that our trading partners abide by their international commitments, ITA provides U.S. businesses and workers the opportunity to compete on a level playing field both in the United States and abroad.

With respect to our trade remedy laws, our AD and CVD investigations are conducted in a fair, objective and transparent manner and in accordance with U.S. law and our international obligations. U.S. AD and CVD proceedings afford all interested parties involved the opportunity to participate and defend their interests. Enforcement of the trade remedy laws plays an important role in supporting the USG's goal of advancing a progressive trade agenda.
As of July 7, 2014, ITA maintains the following AD and CVD orders and ongoing investigations with respect to India:

July 2014	Antidumping	Countervailing	Products
India Orders	14	8	Consumer goods, paper products, steel products, agricultural/aquaculture products, and chemicals
India Investigations	3	3	Various steel products

---

[3] Reorganization Plan No. 3 of 1979, which amended 19 USC Sec. 2171 (describing the functions of the United States Trade Representative under the Trade Act of 1974), assigns the Secretary of Commerce "general operational responsibility for major nonagricultural international trade functions of the United States Government, including...monitoring compliance with international trade agreements to which the United States is a party."

In addition, ITA helps U.S. businesses, including small and medium-sized companies, overcome foreign government-imposed trade barriers to gain access to and fair treatment in India, as well as to the rest of the world. ITA monitors foreign governments' compliance with trade agreement obligations and engages with these governments when problems arise. This includes working closely with U.S. producers and exporters subject to foreign trade remedy actions to track their interactions with the foreign administrating authorities. For example, ITA supported Diebold, a Canton, Ohio-based manufacturer of automated teller machines (ATMs), in its efforts to gain duty free access to India's information technology (IT) sector. India had determined to not classify Diebold's machines as the type of machines eligible for duty free access under the WTO Information Technology Agreement, subjecting them instead to duties of 30 percent. ITA, in cooperation with other U.S. Government agencies, intervened successfully in dialogue with the Indian Commerce and Finance Ministries asking them to reconsider this decision. As a result, India re-classified the machines, reducing the tariffs Diebold owed from 30 percent to zero, and giving it continued duty-free access to an over $100 million market.

Foreign Direct Investment (FDI)

While our trade promotion activities are pivotal to improving the U.S. economy, inward investment also contributes significantly to job creation and economic growth. ITA is seizing this potential and has been working diligently around the world to let investors know that the United States is open for business. In total, U.S. subsidiaries of foreign companies accounted for one-fifth of total U.S. exports, showing the important relationship between trade and investment. In 2012, Indian companies' stock of FDI in the United States was valued around $9.0 billion.[4] Between January 2003 and May 2014, 331 investment projects were announced by Indian firms in the United States, led by the following sectors: software and information technology services, business services, financial services, plastics, and industrial machinery.[5] Conversely, as of 2012, U.S. FDI into India was valued at more than $28 billion.[6]

While India is not our largest source of FDI, it has great potential. In terms of average annual growth over the past five years, India is the eighth-fastest growing source of FDI in the United States, with a compound annual growth rate of 17.8 percent.[7] U.S. subsidiaries of Indian firms employed over 45,100 U.S. workers in 2011, with an average yearly salary of $64,922. U.S.

---

[4] U.S. Bureau of Economic Analysis, *Historical-Cost Foreign Direct Investment Position in the United States and Income Without Current-Cost Adjustment, by Country of Foreign-Parent-Group, 2012, by UBO (Ultimate Beneficial Owner)* (Accessed July 3, 2014)

[5] Source: FDIMarkets.com

[6] U.S. Bureau of Economic Analysis, *U.S. Direct Investment Position Abroad on a Historical-Cost Basis: Country Detail by Industry, 2012* (accessed July 3, 2014).

[7] Calculated from U.S. Bureau of Economic Analysis, *Historical-Cost Foreign Direct Investment Position in the United States and Income Without Current-Cost Adjustment, by Country of Foreign-Parent-Group, by UBO (Ultimate Beneficial Owner)* (Accessed July 3, 2014) – by UBO (Ultimate Beneficial Owner)

subsidiaries of Indian-owned firms have invested $39 million in research and development in the United States, and in 2011, they contributed more than $1.9 billion to U.S. goods and service exports.[8]

The United States is the world's largest free and open market with a longstanding open-investment policy. SelectUSA is the federal-level resource for firms and U.S. economic development organizations (EDOs) and acts as the only U.S. Government-wide program to attract, retain, and grow business investment in the United States. In 2013, the Department of Commerce hosted the SelectUSA Investment Summit. The Investment Summit connected 1,300 participants, including 456 foreign or multinational firms, with more than 200 EDOs. India was one of the largest delegations with a total of 39 investor participants.

SelectUSA, while relatively new, has proven to be a successful program and has had direct success in working to attract India-based investment to the United States. For example, on May 1, 2014, North Carolina Governor Pat McCrory announced that Shri Govindaraja Textiles Private Limited (SG Mills) will open its first U.S.-based operation in Eden, North Carolina, investing more than $40 million and creating 84 jobs over the next two years.
Based on the success of last year's summit, SelectUSA is organizing its second Investment Summit, to be held on March 23- 24, 2015 in Washington, DC.

Conclusion

The United States remains actively engaged in India. The ITA will continue to expand our contacts with the new government in New Delhi, with the Indian state governments – where so many decisions are made -- and with U.S. and Indian businesses and business organizations in order to promote exports of U.S. goods and services. We are looking forward to enhancing this relationship with the upcoming U.S.-India Strategic Dialogue (SD) and other forums where we can actively engage with the Indian government.

---

[8] Anderson, Thomas, *U.S. Affiliates of Foreign Companies: Operations in 2011, Survey of Current Business*, August 2013, U.S. Bureau of Economic Analysis, http://www.bea.gov/scb/pdf/2013/08%20August/0812_us-affiliates.pdf

Mr. CHABOT. Thank you very much. We appreciate your testimony. Members will have 5 minutes now to ask questions, and I will begin with myself.

Ms. Biswal, Secretary Kerry is scheduled to represent the U.S.-India Strategic Dialogue next week. As you are aware, in the past this dialogue has faced some challenges. Can you tell us what issues Secretary Kerry plans to discuss and how the administration will use this opportunity to engage with the new Modi administration on longstanding challenges in our trade and security relationship?

Ms. BISWAL. Thank you, Mr. Chairman.

We do see a very important opportunity in the Strategic Dialogue which will take place in New Delhi next week to be able to relaunch the relationship and, also, put some extraordinary focus on some of the key opportunities, certainly the economic relationship and reinvigorating the trade and investment, looking at some of those issues, but also looking at energy cooperation, including civil nuclear energy, looking at the security relationship and counterterrorism.

And then, we will have a visit shortly thereafter by Secretary Hagel to look at the defense relationship and also put some emphasis on where we want to go together in that aspect of the relationship.

We also see a tremendous opportunity to engage with India on the region and looking at the transition in Afghanistan, looking at the broader Asia landscape, the relationship, and the trilateral dialogue that we have with Japan, and to focus on all of the different aspects of U.S. and India across the Asian landscape. So, we look forward to jump-starting all of those conversations during the Secretary's visit next week.

Mr. CHABOT. Thank you very much.

Let me follow up, Ms. Biswal, on another issue. New Delhi has given Russia's aggression in Crimea implicit approval and strongly opposed sanctions on Moscow, calling Moscow's interest in Crimea "legitimate." Can the U.S. trust India to be a reliable partner on significant geopolitical challenges, if for example, we can't get India's support on this growing crisis? And has the Malaysian airliner shootdown changed India's attitude at all in this particular area?

Ms. BISWAL. You know, I think that is an important issue and an important question. Clearly, India has its own history and its own relationships that guide its foreign policy. But our belief is that the more that we are able to closely consult on these critical issues and challenges that we face around the world, that we hope that we can bring closer together our perspectives and align efforts as much as possible.

We do make the point to our Indian colleagues, as we do to friends around the world, about our perspectives, particularly with respect to Russian aggression in the Ukraine and the implications that that has. And we will continue to have those conversations with India and with other partners around the world.

Mr. CHABOT. All right. Thank you. As chair of this committee and as a Member of Congress, I would consider myself to be very pro-India, but their attitude on this matter with respect to Russia is very disappointing to say the least. I think a lot of other members would probably agree on that.

Mr. Kumar, let me turn to you now. I only have 1½ minutes left. But the High Technology Cooperation Group, chaired by the Department of Commerce, is dedicated to promoting and facilitating bilateral high-technology commerce. Still, many U.S. businesses are facing severe barriers, such as patent revocations and compulsory licenses and copyright piracy and local manufacturing requirements, as I mentioned in my opening remarks. Has the Department of Commerce used this forum to address any of these issues to date? And could you comment in general on those issues?

Mr. KUMAR. Mr. Chairman, we use various conversations, various forms to address exactly these issues that concern our exporters, issues of intellectual property protection, localization issues, where our point of view is that India will actually do better by focusing on having competitive manufacturing as opposed to forcing localization. So, these are all topics that we discuss with them all the time, including during my visit last week.

Mr. CHABOT. Okay. Thank you. Thank you very much.

I am going to stop at that point. I have a little bit of time left. But I am going to now recognize the gentleman——

Mr. CONNOLLY. Mr. Chairman, would you yield in your 25 seconds?

Mr. CHABOT. I will be happy to.

Mr. CONNOLLY. I want to just totally associate myself with your remarks with respect to the Crimea. And I have to say to the Assistant Secretary, I assume the United States' position is this is sovereign territory that was illegally annexed by Russia, and I hope that was clearly conveyed to the new Indian Government. To me, this is not an ambiguous issue or something subject to debate. It is the sovereign territory of the Ukraine and remains so.

I thank the chair.

Mr. CHABOT. I am happy I yielded to you.

The gentleman from New York, who is the ranking member of the full committee, is recognized at this time for the purpose of making a statement.

Mr. ENGEL. Well, thank you, Mr. Chairman. I will be very, very brief.

First of all, I want to thank our two witnesses. Thank you both for your service to our country. It is very much appreciated.

To Mr. Faleomavaega, welcome back. It is good to see you, Eni.

And let me just say that I feel so strongly about the U.S.-India relationship. I was an original member of the India Caucus back in 1990, when we formed it in Congress. And I have often felt that it is a shame that the United States and India through the years hadn't aligned itself more closely.

I know during the Cold War there were some difficulties because India had a close relationship with the Soviet Union, and that kind of made it difficult. But now I really think that both countries should do whatever they can to work more closely together. Our interests are aligned, whether it involves the fight against terrorism or China's rise or just trade. I just think it makes so much sense.

So, I wanted to thank you, Mr. Chairman, for holding this important hearing today. And you can certainly count on me as a friend of India. And I look forward when the Prime Minister comes here in September to greeting him. I think his election also presents us with a tremendous opportunity.

So, again, thank you. Thank you both, and thank you, Mr. Chairman.

Mr. CHABOT. Thank you very much, Mr. Engel.

I now recognize Eni Faleomavaega, the ranking member of this committee, for 5 minutes.

Mr. FALEOMAVAEGA. Thank you, Mr. Chairman.

Secretary Biswal, welcome back. Thank you for being here with us today. I have great hope that you will play an important part to work together to restore our U.S.-India relations.

Your background as a former professional staffer of the House Foreign Affairs Committee and also the unique perspective you have as a member of the Indian-American community I believe is a long-awaited combination that will help bolster relations that have lacked for too long.

Madam Secretary, what do you foresee in this administration's top priorities for strengthening our U.S.-India relationship?

Ms. BISWAL. Thank you, Mr. Faleomavaega.

You know, for India to be the power and reach the potential as a strategic power across the Asia region and across the globe, its first order of business will be revitalizing its economy. And we have a deep interest in partnering with India in that quest and partnering with Prime Minister Modi in that quest.

I think that Prime Minister Modi comes in with strong wind at his back from the business community and confidence from the investor community about the plans that he has outlined and the vision that he has outlined for India's growth.

We think that the United States, that American companies will bring a tremendous amount of technology and support to be able to help that, and we look forward to doing that.

We also think that, as India's economy rises, that India will be increasingly a consequential player across the Asia region, and we think that that is aligned with our interests. We have shared goals and objectives, and we like to see that not only do we have shared goals and objectives, but that we work closely together in achieving those goals, because we will have far greater impact across the region and around the world when we align and work together.

Mr. FALEOMAVAEGA. Secretary Kumar, your background is very impressive. You come to us with extensive global experience in the business world as an Indian-American financial consultant, highly-regarded advisor, and a Silicon Valley entrepreneur.

You are also a poet. I love poems, too. My favorite poet is Rabindranath Tagore.

Prime Minister Modi also is a poet, by the way. I believe poets view the world in a rare and distinct way. From your perspective, Secretary Kumar, both as a poet and as a business leader, what initiatives do you think the United States Department of Commerce should undertake to encourage private sector investment and to advocate for better market access for U.S. exporters?

Mr. KUMAR. Ranking Member Faleomavaega, thank you very much for that very interesting question, combining two different sides of my life.

But let me address that really from the Department of Commerce. We are very active in India with about 70 people on the ground in seven offices, and we are focusing on areas that are of importance to India as they revitalize the economy, to use a term that my colleague has stated. So, our view is to work with the Indian Government and the private sector business in India and here to contribute to that journey.

Mr. FALEOMAVAEGA. I know my time is getting short, Mr. Chairman, but it is certainly good to see Dana here with us also.

You know, for the past years, I have always complained about the fact that we did not seem to pay attention to the Asia-Pacific Region from previous administrations. And I am concerned about it even in this administration. The fact that two-thirds of the world's population is in the Asia-Pacific Region, the fact that our economic interests are just as important and critical in dealing with the Asia-Pacific Region, and I am very concerned.

I know my time is up, Mr. Chairman. Thank you. Appreciate it.

Mr. CHABOT. Thank you very much. The gentleman yields back.

The gentleman from North Carolina, Mr. Holding, is recognized for 5 minutes.

Mr. HOLDING. Thank you, Mr. Chairman.

First, a housekeeping matter. Secretary Biswal, if you could please outline what the State Department has been doing with regards to the jailing of Amway CEO Bill Pinckney? I believe he has been in jail now for 2 months and being held without bail. So, if you could detail that concisely, please?

Ms. BISWAL. Thank you, Congressman.

This has been an issue of very active engagement by the State Department, by our colleagues in the Commerce Department, and really across the U.S. Government. We have worked very closely and intensively with our colleagues in the Indian Government to address piece-by-piece all of the different aspects that stand in the way in achieving bail, hearing, and release on bail for Mr. Pinckney.

We think that, while there may be concerns that the Indian law enforcement have, that no individual should be in jail for 2 months without bail. We think that that needs to be remedied and rectified as soon as possible.

We believe we are making some tremendous progress, and we hope that we will have some very good news on that front soon. We have been working closely with our colleagues at Amway to make sure that we understand all of that, as well as having consular visits to Mr. Pinckney regularly by our Consul General in Hyderabad to make sure of his welfare and make sure that his needs are being addressed.

Mr. HOLDING. Good. Thank you. And if you could keep us abreast of any developments in that, I would appreciate it.

Ms. BISWAL. I would be happy to.

Mr. HOLDING. I will address this to both of you regarding, first, to Secretary Biswal, what damage do you believe that the denial of a visa to then-Chief Minister Modi and the subsequent policy of the State Department that he has to apply in order to find out whether he would be approved or denied again, what damage do you think this has caused our relations with the Prime Minister?

Now I realize that, as a matter of course, as Prime Minister, he is granted a visa as a head of state to come here. But I want to back up to the other issue of him as an individual being not granted a visa, kind of left in this limbo, especially considering the fact that he was cleared by the Supreme Court of India of any of the allegations made against him, which were the basis of the original denial of the visa.

Ms. BISWAL. You know, Congressman, I would say that the administration is very much looking ahead, looking forward, and looking to the future in terms of building a very strong partnership with the Prime Minister and with his team, and strengthening the relationship between the United States and India. We think that we are on a path to do that.

The President called Prime Minister Modi on the day that election results were announced and promptly established——

Mr. HOLDING. I realize that, but I don't believe the State Department has changed its position that, if Mr. Modi were to apply, he would have to apply for a visa to figure out if he was going to get a visa as an individual. Don't you think there ought to be an affirmative statement by the State Department or this administration that they recognize that he has been cleared of these allegations by the Supreme Court of India and that is lifted?

Ms. BISWAL. I would just note that when the President invited Prime Minister Modi and welcomed him to come to the United States, that he did so knowing that visa would be granted for him to be able to do that. And we look forward to that.

I think that we have always made clear for any individual that visa issues are determined on a case-by-case basis. That is not unique to the situation with the Prime Minister.

But we look forward to welcoming him here and——

Mr. HOLDING. I do believe it is unique with Mr. Modi that he is the only individual ever to be denied a visa under the particular clause that he was denied a visa under.

Ms. BISWAL. And I would just say that, while that was the incident that occurred in 2005, that since then there has been no application and there has been no review or determination. And so, there has been no hypothetical basis on which to make a determination.

But we have definitively said that we welcome the visit of the Prime Minister. And therefore, we don't believe that there is any further issue to be addressed with respect to that. I think the President has——

Mr. HOLDING. One final—and I will throw this out to both of you—has there been any statement by the Modi administration, by the Prime Minister himself or people in the administration, about the intellectual property and any perhaps changes to the intellectual property system in India to further align it with our intellectual property protections here in the United States?

Mr. KUMAR. Congressman, I am not aware of any formal statements yet, but we have had conversations in my visit last week with a number of officials in the Indian Government about this topic and about a need to have a constructive dialogue on this topic.

Mr. HOLDING. Well, if you could prospectively maybe keep us apprised of that, members of the committee who are also on the Judiciary Committee and follow these intellectual property issues closely, it would be helpful.

Thank you, Mr. Chairman. I yield back.

Mr. CHABOT. Thank you very much. The gentleman's time has expired.

The gentleman from California, Mr. Bera, is recognized for 5 minutes.

Mr. BERA. Thank you, Mr. Chairman.

In my opening comments, I talked about the time for opportunity. As I think about the Indian-American community here—and my parents immigrated here in the 1950s—in the past decades the Indian-American diaspora has made remarkable accomplishments here in America in a country of opportunity.

So, the excitement of the elections in India that occurred, you feel that same ripple of excitement about the opportunity to create this partnership. It is exciting. As the only Indian-American Member of Congress, it is exciting to see two Assistant Secretaries sitting there from the community. So, this is a time of opportunity.

I do think the administration has reached out immediately, has been very welcoming to the new Prime Minister, and really does reflect that opportunity. And vice versa, Prime Minister Modi ran on an agenda of reviving economic growth in India, building infrastructure in India, and realizing India's full potential as a partner.

And a partnership is a two-way street. So, I think we are going to see a solid foundation. In the next 2 months it will be exciting with three Secretaries visiting, Secretary Kerry, Secretary Pritzker, and Secretary Hagel. I think that offers to lay a foundation for this economic relationship and the geopolitical relationship.

And then, that leads into the September visit of the Prime Minister, and I am excited that I, along with our colleagues, have really pushed the Speaker to extend an invitation to a Joint Session of Congress, which I do think allows us to continue moving forward.

My questions, I think I will start with Assistant Secretary Kumar. When I was in India last year talking to Indian multinationals, and as they visit here in Washington, DC, an untold story is the Indian foreign direct investment here in the United States and the jobs that those create.

With the energy renaissance we are seeing here in the United States, many of the Indian companies that are manufacturing products to sell here in the domestic market really see an opportunity to make those investments and build those factories here in the U.S. From your perspective, what should we do to set the table for more of that foreign direct investment?

Mr. KUMAR. SelectUSA is a program that I mentioned. We are very active in India in promoting investment from India into the U.S. The current level of investment from India to the U.S. is about $9 billion. This covers a wide variety of industries.

In fact, just to mention one from your State, we have a company that recently invested to build an electric two-wheeler. It was developed in Palo Alto, and it is going to be manufactured in Ann Arbor, Michigan.

Another example from the State of North Carolina is an Indian textile company is creating a unit in North Carolina that will create jobs in North Carolina.

So, we are very encouraged by the interest of Indian companies. As they go global, they see the U.S. as the best place to invest. They see the U.S. as a place that provides a global platform to go to other countries. And I am looking forward to seeing more investment from India.

This coming week, in fact, next week, before we go to Delhi, before Secretary Pritzker goes to Delhi for the Strategic Dialogue, she lands in Mumbai and will have a signing ceremony for an agreement with the Ex-Im Bank of India for them to support Indian companies investing in the United States. So, this is a great example of two-way economic relationships.

Mr. BERA. Absolutely. And from our perspective, you know, when we look at India's demographics, it has a very young population. I think one of the assets we have is our system of higher education, our system of community colleges.

And maybe I will direct this question to Assistant Secretary Biswal. I think there is a very real opportunity for our institutions of higher learning to help develop a similar system in India to educate/train that workforce to realize a very unique asset to India.

Your thoughts?

Ms. BISWAL. Absolutely, Congressman. I would just note on your previous question I just want to make the comment that Indian investment in the United States has also resulted in over 100,000 jobs in the United States. So, I think that that is a powerful example of the two-way trade and the two-way benefits of this relationship.

With respect to skills in higher education, this is a big priority for the Modi government. The Prime Minister raised this in his meeting with Deputy Secretary Burns. It is an active area of engagement through our higher-education dialogue. We are looking at not only how U.S. institutions of higher education, our universities, can partner with India, both in terms of Indian students studying in the United States as well as opportunities to expand access to education in India.

The other major aspect that we are looking at is a community college initiative, how the very excellent community college system in the United States, which really expands access to higher education to so many millions of Americans, how that system can also partner with India to advance access to vocational education and skills for an Indian workforce that is increasingly going to be needed for India's economy to grow.

Mr. CHABOT. The gentleman's time has expired.

The gentleman from Florida, Mr. Clawson, is recognized for 5 minutes.

Mr. CLAWSON. Having invested tens of millions of dollars in India myself, I have a little bit of understanding of your challenges and the opportunities. I always felt glad that I had a good partner, Bharat Forge, because India scared me. The bureaucracy scared me. The regulations scared me. The currency controls didn't even seem fair. The import tariffs didn't seem fair. It felt like my capital could flow in, but my profits could not flow out. And it felt like

34

product from India can flow out, but product into India cannot flow in easily. In today's world where capital generally has no barriers, it didn't feel like a totally modern system. And so, therefore, I was glad that I had a very good partner who could help us through it. Otherwise, we may not have made the investments.

As I see a new regime take hold in India, one who feels at least at the start to have a modern view of the world and a modern view of accounting, is this administration now committed to eliminating some of the currency regulations, import barriers, bureaucracies, and controls that make business one-sided and difficult for those that want to invest?

Mr. KUMAR. So, Congressman, this is an important topic for us. I was in India, as I mentioned, last week meeting with officials, which was the first time we were meeting with the new government. And in all our conversations we talked about the importance of a new business climate, a climate that addresses exactly those kinds of issues that you talked about.

India is interested in more investment to create jobs, and these are exactly the kinds of points that we will be making in our conversations with the Government of India and with the private sector and other stakeholders in India.

Ms. BISWAL. So, I would just add to that to say, Congressman, that while we see some very hopeful signs, and the budget that was put out, the interim budget that was put out by the new government, was certainly a step in the right direction, that this is going to be a process that is going to have to unfold. And so, we look forward to continuing to see what steps the government takes to liberalize its economy and to attract greater trade, greater investment, which are all their stated objectives.

Mr. CLAWSON. I am glad that India companies invest in the United States, and only private investment produces good-paying jobs. Governments do not. And capital votes by walking.

And so, therefore, I would just like American businesses to have the same fair shake in India that Indian businesses have here. That has been the ongoing relationship that will be of interest to me, because I think fairness for our country—our trade deficit is hundreds of billions of dollars. And some of that is artificial and it doesn't have to be there.

So, just as your capital is welcome here to produce good-paying jobs in the U.S., I would like our capital to be welcome there, and there to be freedom of capital, so that both sides are on the same territory. And I ask cooperation and commitment and priority from your government in so doing. Can I have that?

Ms. BISWAL. I think your question is to the Indian Government, and we certainly share your sentiments. We certainly will advocate that on behalf of the U.S.——

Mr. CLAWSON. Of course. And I am asking your opinion of how they view that.

Ms. BISWAL. Like I said, I think we have heard a lot of very positive signals, a lot of positive intentions, and we will be engaging both through the State Department, through the Commerce Department, through our USTR, through our Treasury Department, to make sure that we are engaging on those issues and looking for the concrete steps forward.

Mr. CLAWSON. Okay. Let's see some progress.

Ms. BISWAL. Absolutely.

Mr. CHABOT. The gentleman is finished?

Mr. CLAWSON. Yes.

Mr. CHABOT. Okay. Thank you very much.

Mr. CLAWSON. I yield back.

Mr. CHABOT. The gentleman's time has expired.

I assume that the members heard the bells ringing, but we just have two more members. So, we should be okay with 5 minutes each. The gentleman from the Commonwealth of Virginia, Mr. Connolly, is recognized for 5 minutes.

Mr. CONNOLLY. I thank my chair.

And I would just say to our newest colleague, I would be glad to take you to my district. Government does create high-paying jobs. The three wealthiest counties in the United States are the wealthiest counties in the United States; they are all in Northern Virginia. Two of them are in my district. And it is because of the unique partnership between the Federal Government and the private sector in high tech, R&D, and defense contracting. The government most certainly does create good-paying jobs, at least in my part of the world. It isn't just the private sector.

I might also add that an awful lot of what has transformed the world was entirely a government investment. The idea that the government can do nothing right is nonsense. Look at GPS technology, 100 percent a Federal investment; the internet, 100 percent, called DARPANET, for 25 years a government-funded investment, not a dime of private sector investment. And it transformed the world.

This notion that somehow the government can't do anything right or, you know, it needs to just get out of the way, is not true. And at least my private sector and my chambers of commerce recognize how valuable and vital that partnership is here in America, and I assume it is also true in India.

Ms. Biswal, I wanted to give you a chance because, unfortunately, I took advantage of the 25 seconds left to the chairman. You wanted to comment on Crimea, and I wanted to give you that opportunity.

Ms. BISWAL. Only, sir, that we certainly agree wholeheartedly with your characterization and we continue to engage with our Indian friends to ensure that they understand our perspective. As I said, we strive to continue to bring our perspectives closer in alignment.

Mr. CONNOLLY. Thank you. I wanted to give you that opportunity and I appreciate it, especially since you had the good sense to go to the University of Virginia and you were a staffer. I, too, was a staffer.

I also want to identify myself with the remarks of Ami Bera, my good friend from California, who talked about the U.S.-India relationship perhaps being the defining relationship of the 21st century. I couldn't agree more. I think that India is such an important potential partner, and we with India. I think it is actually potentially much more important than the Chinese relationship.

We have lots in common. You know, we share a lot of language together. We have many common values. We certainly share democratic values in common.

And I wonder if either of you would like to comment on that, because I think there are lots of prospects and I am very hopeful that, with the Modi visit here to Washington, we can cement some of those values and those relationships to move forward.

Ms. BISWAL. You know, fundamentally, India's rise and India's democratic growth, democratic development, is a very important aspect not only in terms of what it represents in terms of opportunities for partnership, but it is also very important in terms of the example that it sends to the other emerging and developing economies around the world that democratic development does result in strong growth, inclusive growth, and opportunities for these countries. And I think that India represents that, and India's success with that model is very much in the U.S. interest and that defines in many ways the core values of our partnership.

Mr. CONNOLLY. Mr. Kumar?

And then, Mr. Chairman, I am going to yield the balance of my time to Ms. Gabbard.

Mr. KUMAR. Yes, I would just reemphasize the importance of India's growth to our people. If you look at the last few years, U.S. exports stagnated when India's growth stagnated. Years before that when India was growing, when it even passed double digits, U.S. exports to India grew significantly. So, we are very aggressive in India's growth because that directly helps our people here who can export more, and we create jobs as a result here.

Mr. CONNOLLY. Thank you. And I yield the balance of my time to Ms. Gabbard.

Mr. CHABOT. The gentlewoman from Hawaii is recognized.

Ms. GABBARD. Thank you very much, Mr. Chairman, Mr. Connolly.

Thank you both for being here. It is great to see you, as always.

I will keep this brief. A lot of great points have already been brought up. My questions will really be more on the opportunity for us in the security partnership front with India.

I think that recognizing the opportunity that exists with this change of leadership in India must be seized by us in a way that is very proactive and sensitive to what has occurred in the past, and done in a way that India understands that we greatly value the opportunity for both of our countries as we move forward.

I am wondering if you can just speak a little bit about what the security cooperation is that we look forward to achieving, especially as we look at all of the things that are happening in the world and different relationships, but especially as we look at Afghanistan and the path going forward, and India's vested interest in the region, but also India's current presence already across the country of Afghanistan.

Ms. BISWAL. Thank you, Congresswoman.

What I would note is that, shortly after we have the Strategic Dialogue, Secretary Hagel is also looking to go to India in early August. One of the key objectives there is to be able to engage with the Indian Government to map out their priorities in terms of where they want to see the defense partnership go and what we see as the potential, both short-term and long-term, for that relationship.

This is a defense partnership that has seen tremendous growth over the past decade, and we do more military exercises, for example, with India than with virtually any other country. Right now, as we speak, India is participating in the RIMPAC exercises in Honolulu for the first time, and we have the Malabar exercises, which are trilateral this year with India, the U.S., and Japan.

We see great prospects for deepening that cooperation, but we also see that, as India seeks to create a defense manufacturing base and as India seeks to modernize its defense sector, that the United States is going to play a critical role. We seek to deepen that partnership, to look for opportunities for co-development and co-production in that range. Because as India's capacity grows, the ability of India to be a force for stability and security across the Asia-Pacific grows as well, and that is something that we very much support.

With respect to Afghanistan, Congresswoman, we have very close consultations with our colleagues in India about how we see that transition in Afghanistan unfolding. We had an opportunity to have some extensive conversations during the visit of the Deputy Secretary 2 weeks ago. And I know that that is a key aspect for the agenda for Secretary Kerry for his visit next week. We will continue to look for ways that the United States and India and the other countries in the region can work together for stability and security in Afghanistan, which is certainly in the Afghans' interest, but also in the interest of all the countries of the region.

Ms. GABBARD. Quickly, and forgive me if you already talked about this, but what are the prospects of the timeline like for appointing a new Ambassador to India?

Ms. BISWAL. Well, as you know, it is going through its own internal process of the White House. This is a big priority for the administration, for the President. And so, we hope that we can conclude the internal process sometime soon, and then, it will be with the legislative branch for Senate confirmation.

But this is a big priority. It was, therefore, a decision of the administration to place Ambassador Kathy Stephens there as charge'. She is one who brings great skill and experience and expertise, and particularly her experience in East Asia as Ambassador to Korea has been very welcome as well.

Ms. GABBARD. Great. Thank you.

Thank you, Mr. Chairman. I yield back.

Mr. CHABOT. The gentlelady yields back.

I would like to thank the panel for their very excellent testimony this afternoon. I would note that members will have 5 days to revise their statements or submit questions in writing. And if there is no further business to come before the committee——

Mr. FALEOMAVAEGA. Will the chairman yield? I'm sorry.

Mr. CHABOT. Yes, I would be happy to yield to the gentleman.

Mr. FALEOMAVAEGA. I just want to personally thank you again, Mr. Chairman, for your leadership in having this hearing today, and certainly thank our witnesses for coming. I look forward to continuing a good working relationship with you, Mr. Chairman.

Thank you.

Mr. CHABOT. I am committed to that for sure.
And you are welcome.
Thank you.
We are adjourned.
[Whereupon, at 5:09 p.m., the meeting was adjourned.]

APPENDIX

MATERIAL SUBMITTED FOR THE RECORD

SUBCOMMITTEE HEARING NOTICE
COMMITTEE ON FOREIGN AFFAIRS
U.S. HOUSE OF REPRESENTATIVES
WASHINGTON, DC 20515-6128

Subcommittee on Asia and the Pacific
Steve Chabot (R-OH), Chairman

July 21, 2014

TO: MEMBERS OF THE COMMITTEE ON FOREIGN AFFAIRS

You are respectfully requested to attend an OPEN hearing of the Committee on Foreign Affairs, to be held by the Subcommittee on Asia and the Pacific in Room 2172 of the Rayburn House Office Building (and available live on the Committee website at www.foreignaffairs.house.gov):

DATE: Thursday, July 24, 2014

TIME: 3:00 p.m.

SUBJECT: U.S.-India Relations Under the Modi Government

WITNESSES: The Honorable Nisha Biswal
                 Assistant Secretary
                 Bureau of South and Central Asian Affairs
                 U.S. Department of State

                 The Honorable Arun Kumar
                 Director General of the U.S. and Foreign Commercial Service and
                 Assistant Secretary for Global Markets
                 International Trade Administration
                 U.S. Department of Commerce

By Direction of the Chairman

The Committee on Foreign Affairs seeks to make its facilities accessible to persons with disabilities. If you are in need of special accommodations, please call 202/225-5021 at least four business days in advance of the event, whenever practicable. Questions with regard to special accommodations in general (including availability of Committee materials in alternative formats and assistive listening devices) may be directed to the Committee.

COMMITTEE ON FOREIGN AFFAIRS

MINUTES OF SUBCOMMITTEE ON _____ *Asia & the Pacific* _____ HEARING

Day___ *Thursday*___ Date____ *7/24/2014* _____ Room_____ *2172* _____

Starting Time __ *4:00 p.m.*___ Ending Time __ *5:02 p.m.* ___

Recesses |_____| (____to ____)(____to ____)(____to ____)(____to ____)(____to ____)(____to ____)

Presiding Member(s)
Chairman Steve Chabot (R-OH), Ranking Member Eni Faleomavaega (D-AS)

Check all of the following that apply:

Open Session ☑   Electronically Recorded (taped) ☑
Executive (closed) Session ☐   Stenographic Record ☑
Televised ☑

TITLE OF HEARING:
U.S.-India Relations Under the Modi Government

SUBCOMMITTEE MEMBERS PRESENT:
Rep. Ami Bera (D-CA), Rep. George Holding (R-NC), Rep. Curt Clawson (R-FL), Rep. Scott Perry (R-PA), Rep. Doug Collins (R-GA), Rep. Gerald Connolly (D-VA), Rep. Tulsi Gabbard (D-HI), Rep. Dana Rohrabacher (R-CA), Rep. Brad Sherman (D-CA)

NON-SUBCOMMITTEE MEMBERS PRESENT: *(Mark with an * if they are not members of full committee.)*

Ranking Member Eliot Engel (D-NY)

HEARING WITNESSES: Same as meeting notice attached? Yes ☑ No ☐
(If "no", please list below and include title, agency, department, or organization.)

STATEMENTS FOR THE RECORD: *(List any statements submitted for the record.)*
Ranking Member Faleomavaega's Statement for the Record
Chairman Royce's Opening Statement

TIME SCHEDULED TO RECONVENE _____
or
TIME ADJOURNED __ *5:02 p.m.* __

_____
Subcommittee Staff Director

COMMITTEE ON FOREIGN AFFAIRS
U.S. HOUSE OF REPRESENTATIVES
WASHINGTON, D.C. 20515

SUBCOMMITTEE ON ASIA AND THE PACIFIC
ENI F.H. FALEOMAVAEGA (D-AS)
RANKING MEMBER

U.S.-India Relations under the Modi Government

July 24, 2014

Mr. Chairman:

As Prime Minister Modi said, "Good days are coming."

I agree. I am grateful to Heavenly Father for good days – and good friends.

I would be remiss if I did not take this opportunity to personally thank you, Mr. Chairman, and Mr. Bera for your support, thoughts and prayers during my time of recovery. I also thank the Members of this Subcommittee as well as my colleagues in the U.S. House of Representatives.

I am grateful to each of you and very grateful to be back working with you on the important issues facing Asia and the Pacific. I believe together we still have a difference to make.

And so, I thank you for holding this important hearing at my request on U.S.-India relations under the Modi government.

History will remember India's 2014 elections as unprecedented. I will remember the 2014 elections as an epoch triumph because – on May 16, 2014 – in the most historic elections since India's independence – Shri Modi won India in a landslide victory that gave Shri Modi the most decisive mandate for an Indian Prime Minister in three decades despite the United States using every recourse it could to disrupt his destiny.

No doubt, Prime Minister Modi's destiny is to lift up the masses, assure social justice, and bring new hope for any and all who, like him, step forward and transform challenges into opportunities by sheer strength of character and courage

Prime Minister Modi's victory is India's victory. It is our victory, too, and I join with the people of India in celebrating a new dawn of development for all.

The U.S.-India partnership should be, could be, one of the most defining of the 21st century. While it is shameful that the United States failed to develop a strong friendship and comprehensive partnership with Shri Modi when it mattered most, I thank Prime Minister Modi for accepting President Obama's invitation to meet at the White House on September 30 of this year.

Prime Minister's willingness to put the past in the past is a testament to his track record of good governance. He is a selfless leader who puts India first.

In recognition of his visit to our Nation capital, I join with my colleagues in calling upon the House and Senate Leadership to invite Prime Minister Modi to address a Joint Session of the U.S. Congress. I commend the co-chairs of the House Caucus on India and Indian Americans and their counterparts in the Senate, and also Congressman Brad Sherman, Congressman Ami Bera, Mr. Sanjay Puri of the Alliance for U.S.-India Business (AUSIB), and all those who are working together for this purpose.

I also thank Mr. Puri for introducing me to Shri Modi in 2010. In 2010, Shri Modi was Chief Minister of Gujarat and I was Chairman of this Subcommittee. I flew to Gujarat to meet the Chief Minister at his residence. I knew then what I know now. Shri Modi is dedicated. He is determined. He is dynamic. He is different. He is the key player for improved relations between the U.S. and India.

Today he is the leader of the world's largest democracy, and I have every confidence he will cut across caste, creed and religion and bring alive the dreams of over a billion Indians, and a world that needs his leadership. As a man of vision and action, he, together with each and every citizen of India, will create something special – an India of sustainable development and inclusive growth and an India that will rightfully assume its place in the political and economic affairs of this world.

You can be assured Prime Minister Modi will usher in India's new era. And the U.S. would be wise to support his goals. India "will not threaten nor be intimidated by any country." India will deepen partnerships regionally and globally in areas of defense, nuclear energy, space research, and trade and investment. India will also invest heavily in infrastructure, affordable housing, healthcare, education, and clean energy.

India will advance the interests of the developing world and lead the way in establishing a new model for maintaining stability without constraining growth. Prime Minister Modi will devote it all to eradicate poverty.

Good days are coming – no matter the pundits and critics who have too long maligned Shri Modi and his supporters. And so, once more, I congratulate Shri Modi on his path-breaking campaign, and I praise BJP Party President Singh for working shoulder-to-shoulder with Shri Modi to ensure that the spirit of democracy has triumphed.

I also commend Mr. Sanjay Puri for championing the cause and work of Shri Modi in Congress at a time when others were not courageous enough, and for holding firm even though he was also unjustly and wrongly maligned.

Above all, I praise Prime Minister Modi. From his beginnings as a son of a tea seller to a ground-breaking victor, I wish Shri Modi every success on his poetic journey forward as the Prime Minister that the people of India have long-awaited.

PREPARED STATEMENT SUBMITTED FOR THE RECORD BY THE HONORABLE EDWARD R. ROYCE, A REPRESENTATIVE IN CONGRESS FROM THE STATE OF CALIFORNIA, AND CHAIRMAN, COMMITTEE ON FOREIGN AFFAIRS

Asia Subcommittee Hearing: "U.S.-India Relations Under the Modi Government"
July 24, 2014
2172 Rayburn

Opening Statement:

Thank you, Mr. Chairman for holding this important hearing. In every aspect – whether it be in political, economic or security relations – the United States has no more important partner in South Asia. It is not an overstatement to say that the U.S.-India relationship will help define the future of the region. And that is why I was pleased to join my friend and colleague, George Holding, in inviting Prime Minister Modi to address a Joint Meeting of Congress when he travels to Washington in September.

I am optimistic that the mandate given to Prime Minister Modi will help India thrive economically, lifting countless people out of poverty. Having travelled to Gujarat following the devastating 2001 earthquake – a disaster that claimed the lives of 20,000 and injured hundreds of thousands more – I had the opportunity to meet Mr. Modi, and witness firsthand the astonishing reconstruction effort he led. It would have been impossible to imagine then that the district of Kutch, decimated to near rubble, would become an economic boomtown, attracting hundreds of businesses and creating thousands of jobs.

Since that time, Gujarat has flourished. Experiencing an average growth rate of 10.3 percent in the decade since Modi took power, Gujarat outpaced India's overall growth by two percent. Under Mr. Modi's leadership, Gujarat, home to a mere five percent of the country's population, now accounts for nearly 25 percent of all Indian exports. Not surprisingly, poverty rates have fallen dramatically under his leadership.

Like with all partnerships, there are challenges that we can address. In its annual report on global trade, the U.S. Trade Representative said, "U.S. exporters continue to encounter tariff and non-tariff barriers that impeded imports of U.S. products into India," and that restrictions on foreign investment and complex customs procedures continue to deter trade. The new government must tackle these problems.

India has the opportunity to implement important reforms such as the privatization of state-run banks and the relinquishing of the government's control of coal production. Prime Minister Modi's historic victory has granted him a mandate unseen in decades. If Modi is successful, all Indians will have an opportunity to unleash their abundant economic talent and potential, as Gujartis have. He now has the opportunity to reinvigorate India's economy and bring new energy to U.S.-India relations.

Thank you again, Mr. Chairman for holding this important hearing. I yield back the balance of my time.